Accidental Poetess

KATHY SHERBAN

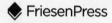
FriesenPress

Suite 300 - 990 Fort St
Victoria, BC, V8V 3K2
Canada

www.friesenpress.com

Copyright © 2021 by Kathy Sherban
First Edition — 2021

All rights reserved.

No part of this publication may be reproduced in any form, or by any means, electronic or mechanical, including photocopying, recording, or any information browsing, storage, or retrieval system, without permission in writing from FriesenPress.

Illustrations by Tyra Schad.

Forward by Colleen McGillicuddy McLaren

Photography by Alydia Hilliard

ISBN
978-1-03-911558-3 (Hardcover)
978-1-03-911557-6 (Paperback)
978-1-03-911559-0 (eBook)

Poetry, Subjects & Themes, Women Authors

Distributed to the trade by The Ingram Book Company

Table of Contents

Dedication ix

Foreword..xi

Endorsements xiii

Preface xv
Accidental Poetess xvii

Acknowledgements xix

Chapter One: SARS-CoV-2 1
1. 2020 Time Capsule.. 3
2. Corona 5
3. Click Bait 6
4. Craziness 7
5. Travel Advisory 9
6. New Order 10
7. Winds of Change.. 12
8. Shopping Protocols.. 13
9. Back to Basics 14
10. New Day 15
11. Covid Cravings 16
12. Backyard Barber 17
13. The Struggle 18
14. Canada Emergency Response Benefit (CERB) 19

15.	Covid "Karens"	21
16.	Entitled	22
17.	Waves	23
18.	Blurred Lines	24
19.	Regional Models	25
20.	Covid Rhetoric	26
21.	Life Continues	27
22.	My Day	28
23.	Emotional Huddles	29
24.	2021 Begins	30
25.	The Legacy	32

Chapter Two: Politi-ques 33

1.	Misconduct	35
2.	Modern Day Crack	36
3.	Fake News	37
4.	Political Warfare	38
5.	U.S. Presidential Election	39
6.	Mr. President	40
7.	Trump-sters	42
8.	Congressional Storm	44

Chapter Three: Heart Beat-Z 47

1.	Trauma	49
2.	The Haunting	50
3.	Secret Society	51
4.	Anxiety	52
5.	Edge of Madness	53
6.	The Ghost	54
7.	Mayday	55
8.	Impetus	56

9.	Bell Let's Talk	57
10.	Acceptance	59
11.	Letting go	60
12.	Today	61
13.	Footprints	62
14.	The Prayer	63
15.	Silent Goodbye	64
16.	Heaven's Gate	65
17.	Grief	66
18.	The Guardian	68

Chapter Four: PEEPs 69

1.	The Village	71
2.	Just Human	72
3.	Birds of a Feather	73
4.	Cautionary Tale	74
5.	Hidden Gem	75
6.	Counterfeit Friend	76
7.	"HER"	77
8.	The Tramp	78
9.	Underdog	79
10.	The Bully	80
11.	Pretty Woman	81
12.	Family Affairs	82
13.	The Elephant	83
14.	Drama	84
15.	Carnage	85
16.	Mother	86
17.	The Parent	87
18.	Chosen Ones	88

Chapter Five: Romantico **89**
1. Romantic Cycle 91
2. Affaire de Coeur 92
3. The Quest 93
4. When Cupid Strikes 94
5. Love Bandit 95
6. Against the Odds 96
7. My Forever 97
8. Date Night 98
9. The Code 99
10. Drowning 100
11. Mr. Wrong 101
12. Toxic Love 102
13. The Love Story 103
14. Emotional Warfare 104

Chapter Six: Life-ism **105**
1. Life according to "L" 107
2. Age of Innocence 108
3. Mind Over Matter 109
4. Rite of Passage 110
5. Life's Journey 111
6. The Exchange 112
7. No Regrets 113
8. Personal Currency 114
9. Giving Back 115
10. It's a Wrap 116
11. OutKast 117
12. One of a Kind 118
13. Perfect World 119

14. The Blast 120
15. Personal Value 121
16. Cheers 122
17. The Lesson 123
18. Point of Origin 124
19. C-Town Central 125
20. Rise Up 127
21. The "Millennial" 128
22. Team Green 129

Dedication

To my husband Adam

Your unconditional love, strength, and constant source of wisdom have lifted me from darkness, carried me through ambiguity, and guided me through storms. YOU are my Rock, my North Star, my Happily Ever After! Without you this book would not have been possible.

To my son Justin

My only child, whom I love more than life, my heart is not whole without you! I am so very proud of the man you have become; you are a constant source of inspiration. Your love and support encourage me to always try to be the very best version of myself.

Foreword

From the outside looking in I grew up with a charmed life. Peer a little closer, tucked neatly away was alcohol abuse, confusion and feelings of being misunderstood.

Perception was Colleen is "deep" however being deep was not a value it was merely an aberration. Feeling vacant and enraged, either the world was crazy or I was.

A high school dropout, kicked out of our family home to later return tail tucked, heartbroken and failed endeavors....

Enter hairdressing, Hairport, my salon on Railway Street in Cochrane, Ontario where creativity, popularity and unbridled fun was enjoyed by all.

In 1980 I hired a young styling assistant named Kathy Moorehead, she was efficient, energetic and savvy beyond her 15 years. A street urchin, she was couch surfing between friends until she could find a permanent arrangement. Beneath her tough exterior was a young, vulnerable, lost soul desperately trying to navigate life. I immediately recognized myself in her....

Living and working in a small-town, co-workers quickly bond and friends become family. Eventually, over time we all spread our wings soaring off in separate directions.

What seems many lifetimes later, came the advent of internet and Facebook. One day I received and accepted a friend request from a woman named Kathy Sherban. Low and behold, it was my old protégé Kathy Moorehead, married, with a family and successful career.

Over time my eyes began to meet with her daily prose, every word seemed to jump from the screen evoking in me strong emotional responses. Rhyming in two to three-word sentences, her delivery is packed with punches, it is raw and direct. Powerfully naked, masterfully crafted, she digs deep into spirituality and mental illness. Her word play evokes immediate hard-hitting pictures of dynamic levels manifesting the human plight. The reader will cry, marvel and laugh when she succinctly nails Corona, a synonym for both beer and covid but without the hangover.

Kathy's poems will spur a gut reaction from anyone who reads them. I urge you to sit back, imbibe every succulent thought she provokes. Don't just read her poetry, inhale it!

Kathy has definitely found her wings, survived and is thriving. She is fabulous, talented, devoid of triviality, sincere, generous, keeps it real and is nobody's fool.

Accidental Poetess is no accident! It is deeply rooted in profound pain, personal healing and immense love. This book of poetry depicts the window into the human condition before the great reset. A MUST read!

Colleen McGillicuddy McLaren
Author, *"I Got This!" The Sisterhood Folios Book #9*

Endorsements

"Kathy's poems are deliciously succinct yet explode with volumes of insight. I am in awe of her ability to pack her perspectives on topics like complex societal issues, current political unrest, or the joys and heartaches of love—into these satisfying little morsels. The Accidental Poetess is packed with poetic honesty that leaves us hungry for more."

Beth Redman Kray
Author, *Life Song Poems*

"I recognized Kathy's fiery passion early in our friendship so I wasn't at all shocked when I began reading her poetry. Her courage and enthusiasm exude in her writing, especially in the face of adversity! Accidental Poetess captured my immediate attention leaving me excited to read more of her work!"

Cindy Huggins-Deveau
Author, *Brave Girl*

"Kathy has a refreshing and entertaining flair for creating thought-provoking poems which are insightfully relevant – no matter the level of poetry aficionado. Whether sitting on

the dock on Buckhorn Lake or riding the subway to your job on Bay Street, you will marvel at her ability to tap into your emotions with her prose."

David McKinstry
Author, *Rebel Dad*

"Kathy was always a social student - a good friend to many, independent and feisty, well spoken, and confident. Her observations of life as she lives it, expressed in her poems, are riveting. Kathy is able to capture the essence of a theme in just a few succinct phrases. Her poetry is powerful, diverse, and always satisfying. She uses words that create pictures in our heads ... that stir memories and emotions ... and leave us wanting to read more. A repeated comment about her poems is: You nailed it again!"

Ann Amendola
Kathy's former Gr.5 and Gr.8 teacher

"A wonderful collection of poems that offer a clever commentary on current events and inciteful reflections of her personal experiences and emotions."

Jancis Sullivan
Former Colleague

"Kathy's Accidental Poetess has been my poetry awakening! A must read for poetry lovers and skeptics alike!"

J.P. William (Bill) Galle
New Poetry Buff

Preface

The year 2020 brought about unprecedented change both personally and globally. After many difficult years of silent struggles, I had been recently diagnosed with depression and PTSD. The onset of the global pandemic added to my fragile emotional state. I found myself, like many others, unemployed, restless, lonely, and bored. As a direct result of these circumstances, a new talent emerged that provided me a creative outlet to stimulate my overactive brain; I began writing poetry for the first time in my life. The formation of this perfect storm gave birth to *Accidental Poetess*.

This book is a representation of my authentic self, including my feelings, personal experiences, and observations of various events as they occurred throughout my life. As someone who came from a small northern town, transitioning to the city at a very young age was a challenge. Like many before me, I struggled to adapt and carve out a niche for myself. I did not always get things right the first time around. Self-educated, my survival instinct played a key role in propelling me forward throughout all the various stages of my life. From Cochrane to Toronto's Bay Street to the

Kawartha Lakes, these collected poems are emotional reflections, fond memories, humorous musings, and at times a sad reminiscence of events both past and present.

Accidental Poetess

Melodic rhymes
A lyrical verse
Creative pursuit
A gift or curse
Flood gates erupt
Ideas flow
Concepts collide
Fledgling maestro
Looping sentences
Stringing words
Phonetic metering
Lines are blurred
Literary art
A cathartic release
Poetry in motion
An amateur piece
Abstract stories
Tales to impart
Accidental Poetess
Beats from my heart

Acknowledgements

Funny thing about life, you don't always end up at your intended destination. Some might suggest that my road to poetry was happenstance, I would partially disagree. In reflection, my journey to becoming a Poet has been a cumulative process propelled not only by my crazy life experiences and numerous teachable moments, but also the many incredible people who deeply impacted me along the way. Although I discovered my hidden talent later in life, I am able to share it due in part to the unconditional support and encouragement of those uplifting me, and the advent of the pandemic allowing me to step back and focus solely on my creative ability.

This book would not have been possible without my soul mate, best friend and husband Adam. Thank you for your incredible patience, sitting through multiple narrations of the same poem even though poetry isn't really your thing! Your keen eye and intimate knowledge of my heart helped me to bring my vision forward to represent my book and chapter covers. Your countless hours, days, weeks spent on your own while I was completely immersed in purging every single thought, idea and concept in my head are beyond appreciated! You are a selfless human and I love you beyond measure for that and everything else you bring to my life.

When I began writing poetry, I was very tentative and selective about which pieces I shared with my inner circle. I gingerly stepped into the social media arena not sure how well my poems would be received. My dearest friend Colleen McGillicuddy-McLaren, you shone your brilliant light in my direction, reading, commenting, supporting every single piece, even when your own beliefs didn't align with my message. You allowed for our differences and encouraged me to always stay true to myself and continue to share my heart. You gently nudged me forward, challenging me to do better, giving me the confidence to take this giant leap of faith that has given birth to my very first book: Accidental Poetess! I thank you from the bottom of my heart for being my #1 fan and supporter.

I could not proceed without acknowledging the unwavering support and encouragement from my dear lifelong friend Shannon Smith-Lefevre. You and Colleen are truly kindred spirits. Thank you for always reaching out, checking in, encouraging and supporting my poetic efforts. I am grateful to have you in my corner and blessed to have you as my friend.

It behooves me to mention my early supporters, many whom I've known since I was a child growing up in Cochrane, Ontario. Ann Amendola, from a very young age you were not just my grade school teacher, but a revered mentor, guiding light and safe haven during a very difficult time in my life. You have continued to support me through the years, encouraging and cheerleading from afar. Thank you for always believing in me even when I didn't believe in myself. Nancy Cote, Kathy Fleece-McCaul, Lisa Girard-Smith, Sandra Bussiere, thank you for your friendship through the years, supporting my poetry, cheering me on and being my biggest fans. Thank you for sharing this journey with me, I love each and every one of you!

To my soul sisters Carmen Galle and Linda Lim, this book would not have happened were it not for your friendship, love and support. During my darkest days, you have been my beacon of light, providing hope, laughter, inspiration and kindness. I am a better person for having you both as my ride or die, I love you today, tomorrow and forever. Carmen, I would be remiss if I neglected to mention your plus one, Bill Galle, thank you for supporting my poetry, I am proud to be the one to have converted you into a red-neck buff! I am beyond blessed to boast you all as my closest friends and family!

Karen Khan, where do I begin?! Thank you for your kindness, patience, motherly intuition and gentle prodding to help me unlock my truth and own it. Your guidance and wisdom have been a constant source of comfort and support during one of the most challenging times in my life. I am forever in your debt for seeing me through the darkness and into the light. Without your support I would never have been able to express myself with this newly discovered gift of prose.

My dear friend David McKinstry, thank you for opening your home and your heart to Adam and I during the pandemic. Woodhaven Country Lodge offered us peaceful refuge during some very trying times at the beginning of the pandemic. We immediately fell in love with you, Michael and the kiddos! Your support, enthusiasm and encouragement to publish my poetry was pivotal in propelling me forward in this endeavor. You are my silver lining in this pandemic, I couldn't be more grateful for our friendship.

It is very important for me to acknowledge and thank the Morgan Family (Dave and Joanne) of Beachwood Resort in Lakefield for keeping their doors open during the pandemic. During our transition from Toronto to our new home in Peterborough we enjoyed five months of living in this tranquil setting. I was able write an enormous amount of poetry during our stay at the resort and initiated the publication of this book during that time as well. Thank you for your kindness and generosity, I am forever grateful!

Last but certainly not least, I owe a debt of gratitude to Jeremy Hennessee for teaching me so much about the craft of poetry. Your enormous wealth of knowledge in all things music and poetry have been a constant source of learning and inspiration for me over this past year. Your insightful comments & feedback provided me the courage to believe that my poems were more than just happenstance, that I had a natural gift for metrical prose. Most importantly, thank you from the bottom of my heart for being the muse who inspired the title of my very first published book: Accidental Poetess!

Finally, many thanks to my Publishing Specialist and the Friesenpress Team et al for guiding me through my very first book publication! Your patience and knowledge made for many teachable moments that I will be able to bring forward into my future endeavors. I am beyond proud of our collective efforts and the end results!

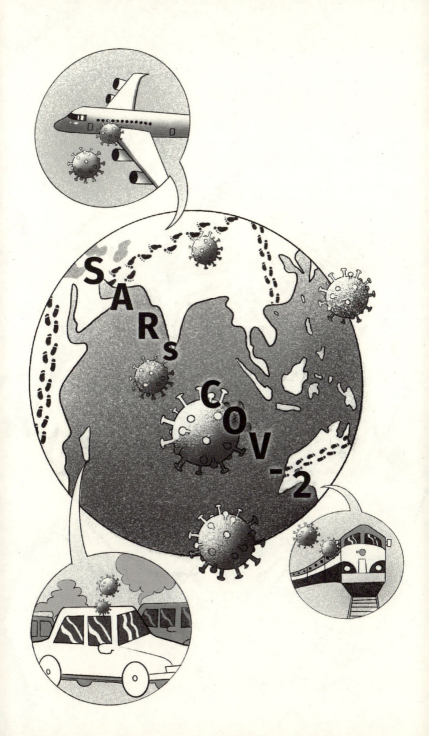

2020 Time Capsule

A year in reflection
major events
Pandemic arrives
efforts to prevent
Covid vaccine
pharma's compete
Pfizer, Moderna
a radical feat
Global lockdown
borders closed
Quarantine Act
restrictions imposed
Olympics postponed
athletes on pause
Japan reschedules
corona's the cause
Presidential impeachment
Trump acquittal
Mueller or Democrats
who to belittle
U.S. election
reason returned
Harris & Biden
lesson learned

Not so fast
chaos ensues
Legal challenges
more fake news
Death of a legend
not to compare
NBA Mamba
a talent so rare
Heartfelt tributes
families torn
Nine lost lives
woefully mourned
Black Lives Matter
movement grows
Antifa rallies
ups the tempo
Protests & Riots
social unrest
Multiple causes
a hornet's nest
Changes abound
turmoil is clear
Beyond profound
the 20th Year

CORONA

Corona with lime
pass me a beer
Party with friends
a drink & a cheer
Consumer warning
brand has a double
Not for enjoyment
this one's trouble
Buyer beware
pandemic is here
Corona's the name
we're not talking beer
Covid 19
a technical term
Terrible illness
killer germ
Give me the hangover
at least there's a cure
Corona alert
virus or beer

CLICK BAIT

Beware the virus
everyone's told
Daily reports
the carnage unfolds
Facebook, Twitter
whatever your source
Nothing's for real
it's bullshit of course
Fact check fiction
where to go
Clickbait stories
who's to know
Politics before science
depends who you ask
Wealth over health
a kick in the ass
Recycled stories
not hard to unmask
A-List networks
now 2nd class
Buyer beware
truth can be skewed
Don't always believe
reports in the news

Craziness

When did it start
How'd it begin
Yesterday's freedom
buried within
Common activity
now a crime
Life got crazy
in such a short time
Cancelled sports
major events
So many folks
can't pay the rent
Scratching my head
state of shock
When did our world
begin to rock
Social assistance
one & all
Never thought
you'd get that call
Unemployed
tired & scared
Hoping bankruptcy
isn't declared

Covid reports
trending each day
Which one matters
More dismay
Life on pause
Hold our breath
One mistake
Life or death

Travel Advisory

Restless wanderers
sit & wait
Backpacking plans
hesitate
Family vacation
one & all
Not this summer
perhaps the fall
Airports, train stations
ports of call
Pedestrian traffic
at a crawl
Online bookings
discount fares
Stay home order
no one dares
Border closures
in effect
Recreational travel
remains suspect
Covid restrictions
Best advice
Social distance
Sacrifice

New Order

Vacant parks
Beaches bare
How'd this happen
Does anyone care
Yellow tape trends
Signs abound
Best think twice
don't mess around
Beyond each corner
Down the street
Bylaw Officers
march their beat
One wrong move
A slight misstep
Ticket written
You won't forget
Socially distance
Neighbours beware
Medically speaking
Not worth the dare
Times have changed
As have you
New rules now
Best to review
It's a new day

Let's be clear
Things will settle
Nothing to fear
Caution is urged
Foot off the gas
Patience folks
This too shall pass

Winds of Change

Empty roads
Quiet streets
Used to wonder
who you'd meet
Cell phone chimes
Message received
Jump right on it
Who could it be
A sign of life
whoever is there
So much alone time
don't even care
Day after day
hours tick by
Seasons change
in the blink of an eye
Sooner than later
this storm shall pass
The winds of change
will arrive alas
2020 began with a roar
What will next year
have in store
The past is a reminder
of yesterdays gone
Over this pandemic
let's move along

Shopping Protocols

Lockdown loosened
don't be fooled
Restrictions remain
just retooled
Premier says go
move very slow
Tory's on board
agrees with Ford
Stores reopen
playbook needed
Strategy's in place
protocols heeded
Shoppers queued
herded in fact
A little too close
major pushback
Two-meter distance
required for all
One-way shopping
be on the ball
Dots on the floor
say no more
Mind your spot
til you're out the door

Back to Basics

Isolation fatigue
boredom mounts
Silver linings
don't discount
New ideas
creative thoughts
Hidden talents
outlets sought
Back to nature
family hikes
Online browsing
shopping spikes
Culinary efforts
innovative cuisine
Traditional recipes
break in routine
Brain teasers
hit the books
Cliff-hangers
totally hooked
Back to basics
reconnect
Express gratitude
introspect
Pandemic blessings
absent strife
Rude awakening
enjoy your life

NEW DAY

Pandemic lessons
new each day
So many changes
here to stay
Common behaviours
second guessed
Wake-up call
we've been blessed
Personal contact
a hug & a kiss
Family, friends
to reminisce
Nails, hair
a stop at the mall
Restaurants, movies
I miss it all
Until it's safe
must be smart
Wave hello
six feet apart
Facetime, Skype
virtual call
Scheduled visits
one & all
Above & beyond
message is clear
Hold very close
those who are dear

Covid Cravings

Hungry again
nothing to eat
Tired of cooking
let's hit the street
Restaurants closed
no food to be had
Grease, fat,
I want what's bad
Burgers, pizza,
street meat, hello
Maybe a combo
I don't really know
Angel, devil,
who's referee
What's the deal
why can't you agree
Cave to the cravings
order it all
Get the menu
make the call
Tummies rumbling
feed the beast
Hurry up Uber
where's my feast

BACKYARD BARBER

Quarantine haircut
needed Fast
Lawn mower
weed whacker
go full blast
Backyard barber
who's the man
Hit me up
fast as you can
Cut or trim
not GQ
Whatever works
gotta be kewl
Urban cowboy
covid clown
Rescue me
from Hippy town

THE STRUGGLE

Global pandemic
domino effect
Society crumbling
much to protect
Federal deficit
provincial debt
Household losses
not over yet
Business closures
shuttered stores
Mass unemployment
hard to ignore
Protocols created
friends disagree
Social distance
herd mentality
Each stage forward
the struggles real
Two steps backward
beyond surreal
The world awaits
life on pause
Vaccine creation
grasping at straws

Canada Emergency Response Benefit (CERB)

Unemployment
business dies
Bankrupt stores
numbers rise
Where's the relief
we need to know
Each passing day
frustration grows
Need some help
step in line
Prepare to wait
It'll take time
Money's coming
Trudeau insists
Folks beware
comes with a twist
Emergency benefits
who can apply
Requirements strict
you must comply
Temporary income
CERB support
Process claim
submit report
Sooner or later
funds are sent

Direct deposit
upon consent
Benefit period
anyone's guess
Cash influx
alleviates stress

Covid "Karens"

Corona shaming
frustration swells
Humans divided
raising hell
Face mask po-po
cover that nose
Wash those hand
don't expose
Criminal treatment
fingers pointed
Social judgement
fears exploited
Trial by peers
bullshit carriers
Verdict rendered
keyboard warriors
Check yourself
mind your own
Covid Karens
bad to the bone
Pandemic protocols
lifestyle choices
Common sense
personal voices
Medical advice
ignore the attacks
Science first
authenticate facts

ENTITLED

Survival instinct
who lives, who dies
Covid capers
on the rise
Pandemic parties
clandestine events
Debbie doubters
circumvent
Vaccine roll-outs
skipping queue
Anti-vaxxers
sceptics argue
Mask meltdowns
dirty deeds
False information
self-interest feeds
He said, She said
biased laws
Letter or Spirit
character flaws
Shady tactics
twisting facts
Misdemeanors
criminal acts

WAVES

Pandemic control
where to begin
Politics & Medics
coordinate a spin
Public announcements
people beware
Next waves here
better take care
Play dates, weddings
parties galore
Rugs been pulled
close that door
Young & old
hefty fines
Social activity
considered a crime
Public conscience
personal test
Stay the course
put covid to rest

BLURRED LINES

Head honchos
drafting rules
Blurring lines
political fools
Colossal fails
two steps back
Bumbling idiots
don't know jack
Chasing tails
dropping balls
Logistical issues
covid protocols
Vaccine rollout
stop the spread
Phased plan
lager heads
Travel mandates
PCR tests
Airlines oblivious
who knows best
Wave three
Ready Set Go
Coming soon
it's a gong show
Swampy leaders
saving face
Into the quagmire
national disgrace

REGIONAL MODELS

Covid fatigue
info overload
Regional model
crack the colour code
Daily reports
efforts a must
Data skewed
who to trust
Protocols plenty
spring thru fall
Record numbers
pandemic snowball
Expanded measures
restrictions imposed
Economy starving
vendors closed
Curbside pickups
lockdown returns
Social gatherings
holiday concerns
Outdoor events
crowds under ten
Repeat directive
stay in your den

Covid Rhetoric

Regional lockdowns
more shops close
Stay home orders
malice exposed
Folks be chirping
stay away
Spend your money
that's ok
Serpent's tongue
lethal beast
Friend or foe
venom released
Pointing fingers
laying blame
Virus or Haters
zero sum game
United we stand
community strong
Check your lane
do you belong
Tolerance triumphs
take deep breaths
Covid rhetoric
the kiss of death

Life Continues

Stay home
common thread
Life's not over
don't be misled
Avoid contact
travel smart
Keep things real
just a start
Herd mentality
not for most
Social distance
covid ghost
Curfews, closures
social distress
Everyone's restless
doing their best
Virus protocols
manage the spread
Avoid the crowds
be a bubble instead
Sooner than later
this too shall pass
Vaccine created
or run outta gas

My Day

Bad hair
don't care
Grey roots
geezer tribute
Spare tire
fat satire
Stretchy pants
Tik Tok dance
Makeup free
shame on me
Fitness time
loafer crime
Meal prep
extra step
Snack attack
cat nap
Day complete
hit repeat

Emotional Huddles

Dial in
call them out
Family, friends
give a shout
In your face
get personal
Mental welfare
critical
Talk, laugh
dirty jokes
Decompress
thought provoke
Cry, bitch
feel the mood
Pep talk
kill the feud
Smile, breathe
huge exhale
Keep it real
no fairy tale
Chill, relax
take it slow
Emotional huddles
don't let go

2021 Begins

A year of change
life transformed
Liberties stripped
global reform
Extreme measures
crisis storms
Virus prevails
variant forms
Mass lockdowns
stop the spread
Restrictions imposed
regional hotbeds
Covid dashboards
data supports
Medical experts
daily reports
Travel advisories
quarantine plans
Contact tracing
use ArriveCAN
PCR testing
negative a must
Vaccine rollout
situational trust
Public spaces
face masks worn
Virus transmission
contagion borne

Social gatherings
two meters apart
School closures
e-learning starts
Online shopping
curbside pickup
Takeout dining
websites develop
Societal impact
economic damage
Covid burnout
much to salvage

The Legacy

Global outlook
fragile at best
Political farce
a personal test
Nature's balance
upside down
Our children's legacy
turn things around
Health & wellness
risk rated high
Pandemic protocols
all must comply
Fiscal deficit
colour me red
Future debt
generational dread
Cause & effect
who's to blame
Societal blinders
wear the shame
Colossal damage
complete disrepair
Millennial's future
begins in despair

Misconduct

Disgraceful behavior, life of a snake
Words used as weapons, not mistakes
Apologies are Band-Aids for reckless hurt
There is no excuse for talking dirt
Stealing from others makes you poor
Dirty deeds won't even the score
Throwing shade reflects worse on you
Lying & cheating completely taboo
Absent honor, the stain of shame
A political life, but a fool's game

Modern Day Crack

My drug of choice
a little Fox News
American politi-ques
radicals amuse
Chaotic interviews
shocking exposés
Mixed reviews
lies on display
Satirical humour
tell-all books
Endless intrigue
this girl's hooked
My daily dose
the inside track
Political warfare
modern day crack

Fake News

Trouble's brewing
watch what appears
The word is out
beware what you hear
Media's on it
news is on fire
Sharing details
the truth we desire
Catch the scoop
how big will this get
Stories so wild
it's not finished yet
Smoke screens prevail
who's to blame
How does this end
Who wears the shame

POLITICAL WARFARE

Democrats or Republicans
red vs blue
Bleeding heart liberals
a capitalist zoo
Political penguins
hot air balloons
Campaign debates
reveal buffoons
Hidden agendas
plans unfold
Promises made
truth gets old
Critical decisions
constituents beware
Choose your evil
better prepare
Elections near
voting's begun
Cast your ballot
declare number ONE

U.S. Presidential Election

Election's over
polls are closed
Winner delayed
division disclosed
Nine states left
Biden or Trump
Neck & neck
pick your chump
The count continues
victory lingers
Who prevails
left- or right-winger
Bated breath
the world awaits
Who's Mr. President
a four-year fate

MR. PRESIDENT

World leader
oath sworn
Public enemy
fabric torn
Dark underbelly
America's pain
Mr. President
claim to shame
False narratives
baseless lies
Breach of trust
zealot vies
Electoral vote
results opposed
Delusional mind
malice exposed
Match lit
bloody hands
Trump's army
loyal lambs
Attempted coup
criminal attack
Chaos & havoc
world reacts

Lock him up
toss the key
Rot in hell
ignore the plea
Expel from office
dude's a bust
Snap impeachment
vote's a must

TRUMP-STERS

Mirror image
friends you keep
True reflection
disciples you seek
Angry mobs
Proud Boyz club
White Supremacists
lawless thugs
Trump supporters
far right wings
Conspiracy theories
Q-Anon sings
Frenemy faves
Kim Jong-un
Letters of love
it's all-in fun
National danger
Putin's the best
Election meddling
be my guest
Israel's finest
Benji the cheat
Corruption charges
man of deceit
Attorney at law
Rudy's the name

Slithering snake
con's his game
Company kept
integrity flies
Standard set
Nobel prize

Congressional Storm

Call to arms
rioters unite
Assault on democracy
dissenters fight
Protesters storm
freak flags fly
Congress breached
America's black eye
Shock & horror
security lax
Insurrection
terrorist attack
Stolen votes
Trump incites
Capital assailed
fire ignites
Chemical agents
people shot
Planned event
nefarious plot
Operational control
curfew imposed
National Guard
Washington closed
Civil unrest

Mr. President speaks
Peace not violence
tongue in cheek
Mentally unfit
oath ignored
Pray for America
order restored

Trauma

The shattering event(s) that create your mold...
That set the stage for your future to unfold...
The story of carnage yet to be told...
The sadly-ever-after for others to behold...

THE HAUNTING

Haunting memories
years gone past
Breaking my spirit
a soul harassed
Emotional scars
a harsh decree
House of horrors
I paid the fee
Each event
a blinding trigger
Flashbacks holler
hello gravedigger
Nightmares persist
rise from the dust
A demon's embrace
forbidden lust
Exorcist needed
kill the ghost
Give me peace
find a new host

Secret Society

Mental health
anxiety & fear
Solitary journey
hope disappears
Covert illness
expertly veiled
Naked truth
a somber tale
Secret society
forbidden club
Caged mind
perceptible snub
Silent battles
veritable storm
Situation critical
needs reform

Anxiety

Heart races
Blood boils
Face flushes
Nails coil
Breathing labours
Frustration surges
Stomach reels
Physical urges
Voice rises
Pinnacle nears
Reason returns
Coast clears
Calm prevails
Panic disappears

Edge of Madness

Shattered mind
devil in disguise
Beckons me home
stifles my cries
Swallows me whole
cheers my grief
Bordering madness
absent relief
Uppers, downers
call the Doc
Medicine cabinet
where's the lock
Climbing walls
sanity's edge
Desperate calls
Lucifer's pledge
Hell's gates
magnetic force
Tormented soul
collision course
Emotional battle
begging for grace
Murky world
temporary space

The Ghost

Silently watching
feeling alone
In a sea of people
even at home
Can't translate
too many secrets
Multiple layers
hard to interpret
A solo journey
life in a bubble
Damaged goods
handful of trouble
A broken child
forever mourned
A tainted woman
woefully scorned
Trapped in the past
no place to roam
A captive mind
in a hostile zone
Shrouded in pain
covering traces
Nobody knows
she has two faces
Coasting thru life
unlike most
Living her life
a translucent ghost

Mayday

Exposed heart
soul laid bare
Lights flickering
a sea of despair
Arms extended
overwrought
Acute fatigue
solace sought
Flare ignited
ill-fated trip
Mayday sent
sinking ship
Darkness settles
hope fades
Salvation pending
emotion's cascade
Search & rescue
lifeline of love
Recovery mission
call from above

IMPETUS

Lift my sadness
grant me peace
My drowning soul
provide release
Shelter my heart
heal the cracks
My dying spirit
medevac
Inner demons
quell my doubt
Eviction notice
toss them out
Dry my tears
stem the flow
Blurry vision
recovery slow
Offer hope
inject faith
Love of life
resuscitate

Bell Let's Talk

Depression lurks
for many each day
A ship in the night
the stowaway
Hidden sadness
protective veil
Shield of armour
visceral jail
Cradled darkness
a lonely retreat
Spiritual bankruptcy
emotional defeat
Mental health
fragile at best
Surrender looms
the ultimate test
Emotional shackles
mental chains
Slippery slope
runaway train
Family or friends
personal bubble
One step back
circumvent trouble
Offer assistance
a shoulder or ear

Course of action
the fog will clear
Help is available
one & all
Bell let's talk
make the call

Acceptance

Emotional intrusions
thoughts & perceptions
Human landmines
cruel intentions
Dodging bullets
chambers loaded
Russian roulette
life eroded
Triggered events
switches flipping
Ready or not
head tripping
Pain, sorrow
rental home
Eviction notice
space to roam
Beefs, grudges
devil may care
Exhale slowly
toxic air
Healing energy
acceptance driven
Heart surrendered
deeds forgiven

Letting Go

Destiny peace
stay the course
Tranquility awaits
feel the force
Process the fear
fight the pain
Nothing to lose
so much to gain
Shift the narrative
gently at first
Negative energy
will be reversed
Serenity's a gift
embraced at last
Long deep breaths
farewell to the past

Today

I live, until death
inhaling each day
Breathing memories
images to replay
Finding nirvana
igniting my core
Absorbing the light
reaching for more
Love & devotion
giving with grace
Gifts & talents
eagerly embrace
Joys of minutiae
defining events
The labyrinth of life
little to lament
Nurture my spirit
food for the soul
Flaws accepted
absolution my goal

Footprints

Lost in reflection
mirror my stage
Silence broken
coming of age
Taste of nostalgia
memories unsealed
Tales of survival
courage revealed
Chronic truant
misbehaved
Double jeopardy
friends betrayed
Fences mended
footprints seared
Former train wreck
passage cleared
Heart healed
pain unpacked
Cycle broken
life on track

The Prayer

I quietly whisper
deep in the night
Praying to God
show me the light
Give me strength
I beg from my bed
Show me grace
i'm hanging by a thread
Take my hand
hold me tight
Lift me up
help me fight
Grant me peace
quiet the storm
Stop the chaos
show me reform
Your divine presence
I give control
Love me forever
protect my soul

Silent Goodbye

Sweeping sadness
melancholy grows
Change so subtle
nobody knows
Mental turmoil
brews within
Emotional storm
about to begin
Sensory overload
feelings collide
Mood shifts
a visceral divide
Body trembles
danger appears
Silent screams
nobody hears
Life or death
a tragic event
Decision made
energy spent

In loving memory of Laura Dekker
December 31st, 1977 - August 9th, 2020

HEAVEN'S GATE

Harps play gently
Heaven opens wide
Angels sing softly
a loved one's arrived
Welcoming arms
family awaits
Into the afterlife
beyond the pearl gates
Sins of the past
all is forgiven
Healing begins
a spiritual transition
Soul surrendered
Our Lord receives
Into eternity
those who believe

In loving memory of John Thomas Moorehead
October 30th, 1959 – December 4th, 2020

GRIEF

Broken hearts
torn & tattered
Crushing pain
lives shattered
Empty vessels
lost in despair
Forlorn hope
beyond repair
Shared stories
memories past
Private agony
shadows cast
Vacant chairs
cooling sheets
Lingering scents
destiny cheats
No goodbyes
sweet farewells
Lost in limbo
gates to hell
Raging anger
consuming grief
Emotional cluster
absent relief
Desperate prayers
sanctity of life

Shedding chains
shackles of strife
Into the darkness
lost in plain sight
A shining star
soul burning bright

In loving memory of my father
Thomas Raymond Moorehead
September 6th, 1942 – December 25th, 2014

The Guardian

I feel your presence
eyes closed tight
I hear your breath
in the quiet of night
Riding shotgun
cavalier
Tapping my shoulder
message is clear
Gently nudging
signal received
My heart cradled
energy perceived
Two souls merged
faith held tight
Joined in tranquility
spirits unite
My rock, my refuge
shrouded in love
My guardian angel
a gift from above

The Village

Each generation
a challenge presents
Struggles to conquer
a future investment
Minds to enlighten
hearts to grow
Faces to brighten
seeds to sow
Tomorrow's voices
leaders born
Modern day warriors
badges worn
Community offspring
foundation laid
Guide to greatness
blood & sweat paid
A collective effort
adults emerge
Confident humans
our forces converge

Just Human

A faulty human
caught in a snare
Best of intentions
not to compare
A heart of gold
tarnished indeed
A broken mold
i'm a dying breed
A gem of a friend
diamond in the rough
Call me soul sister
if things get tough
Forgiveness prevails
acceptance a must
I am just human
in God I trust

Birds of a Feather

Kindred spirits
trusted & true
Absent judgement
right on cue
Ears to listen
hearts that share
Smiles to brighten
people who care
Inside jokes
one of a kind
Pillar of strength
inspirational mind
Straight shooter
honest to a fault
Leads with integrity
designed to exalt
Birds of a feather
soft place to land
Lifetime journey
outstretched hand
Gestures of friendship
year after year
Bonded forever
time disappears

Cautionary Tale

Cocktails & contracts
friendship's waver
Professional transactions
definitely not favors
Business or pleasure
choose your path
Recipe for disaster
colossal aftermath
Errors & omissions
money at stake
Excuse laden emails
forgive my mistake
He said, She said
where lies the blame
Friends & finances
a hazardous game

Hidden Gem

An imperfect woman
faults laid bare
Public judgement
a covert stare
Outer appearance
not much flare
She does her best
why do others care
Beneath the surface
a gem so rare
An inner beauty
enter her lair
Beware your heart
her charm will ensnare
Upon closer inspection
she has much to share

Counterfeit Friend

Into infinity
shallow words flow
Cascading covertly
ever so slow
Carried by wind
a stealthy dart
Deaf ears listen
targeting the heart
Absent candor
deficit is clear
Behind the veil
duplicity appears
Sincerity absent
lip service trends
Beyond the shadows
a counterfeit friend

"HER"

Her gaze
formidable
Intentions
honourable
Her lips
delectable
Scent
excitable
Her aura
celestial
Embrace
irresistible
Her appetite
insatiable
Disposition
unpredictable
Her heart
susceptible
Spirit
unbreakable
Her loyalty
irrefutable
Her love
unconditional

The Tramp

Fruit of the loin
life gets real
Random event
not ideal
Gift or albatross
divine intervention
Decision made
carnal conception
Baby mama
join the queue
Alone & preggers
twenty-two
Broke & jobless
floor's the bed
Radical change
what lies ahead
Unprepared
no dispute
Tarred & feathered
ill repute
Scarlet letter
public stamp
Forever the target
lady's a tramp
Scared & alone
future's uncertain
Reality check
foregone conclusion

Underdog

Fueled by rejection
sparked by love
Driven like the devil
lifted from above
Naysayers persist
passion ignites
One, two punch
begins the fight
Deck is stacked
underdog woes
Human dignity
resilience tiptoes
Quiet confidence
a victor emerged
Sweet success
insecurity purged
Rags to riches
quantified wealth
Personal metric
happiness & health

The Bully

Side-eyed glance
disapproving gaze
Air hangs thick
emotions ablaze
Absent narrative
judgment clear
Silently chastened
openly jeered
Sticks 'n stones
wounds reveal
Scars inflicted
lesions won't heal
Ignorance noted
bullying ignored
Internal bleeding
composure restored
Stiff upper lip
mask in place
Wounds inflicted
smile on my face
Social pariah
vitriol laid bare
Cause & effect
public fanfare

Pretty Woman

Beauty defined
aesthetically pleasing
Scantily clad
forever teasing
Fantasy girl
triple X-rated
Human canvas
fabricated
Surgical implants
fake tans
Hair extensions
chameleons
Optical illusions
nips & tucks
Limited editions
mega bucks
Excess vanity
self-promoted
Eye Candy
sugar-coated
Peer pressure
self-esteem
Model image
a piper's dream

Family Affairs

Gatherings to some
are joyous events
To reconnect
time well spent
Functions to others
are stressful affairs
To carefully avoid
those you beware
Ceremonies for many
are challenging times
To woefully mourn
folks left behind
Family drama
familiar to most
When it occurs
defer to the host

The Elephant

Truth is subjective
depends who you ask
Stories change
lies unmasked
Family secrets
hidden shame
Nobody talks
who's to blame
Seasonal functions
special events
Everyone gathers
despite discontent
Fake smiles
holiday cheer
From the outside in
seems sincere
The cycle continues
with each passing year
At every occasion
the "Elephant" appears

Drama

Day turns to night
stories unfold
Families shattered
tragedy to behold
Broken promises
debacles equal
Just hit repeat
we got a sequel
Hollow words
not worth a penny
A dime a dozen
just too many
Narratives change
falsely framed
Fingers point
shifting blame
Trust broken
hope diminished
Nothing's left
drama's finished

Carnage

You left our world
Christmas day
Your final journey
To our dismay
Shattered hearts
fractured ties
Mass destruction
sad goodbyes
Dark secrets
denials & lies
Shrouded forever
no surprise
A family flawed
deep in despair
Children injured
beyond repair
Hurt & shame
your legacy ends
The cycle broken
truth transcends

MOTHER

Softly "She" whispered
Gently supported
Spiritually lifted
Bravely escorted
Mindfully mentored
Tirelessly cheered
Emotionally championed
Educationally steered
Who is this woman
guiding your flight
"She" is your Mother
your inspirational light

The Parent

Come closer my child
whisper your fear
Help, you beseech
life is unclear
I offer my hand
together we walk
An ear to listen
a time to talk
Teachable moments
wrongs turned right
Each step forward
lessons take flight
United we stand
truth laid bare
Weight offloaded
burden shared
Sense of purpose
life realigns
Together we journey
your pain is now mine

Chosen Ones

Inner circle
solidarity grows
Pedigree blends
trust bestowed
Comrades chosen
allegiance sworn
An eternal bond
family formed
Kindred spirits
sign from above
Flawed humans
imperfect love
God's gift
inside voice
Friends turned family
always a choice

Dedicated to my beautiful "Soul Sisters"
Carmen Galle & Linda Lim

Romantic Cycle

Dating game
teenage crush
Mad obsession
royal flush
Cohabitation
door open wide
Kick to the curb
thanks for the ride
Wedding's a snap
ceremonial bliss
A few simple words
sealed with a kiss
Marital vows
for better or worse
Conjugal bond
blessing or curse
Married life
not for the weak
Stay the course
beware shitz creek
Divorce decree
status reset
Goodbye riches
hello debt
Eternal Love
second chance
Heart's desire
true romance

Affaire de Coeur

Your lingering scent
our smoldering heat
Whispered pleasures
bitterly sweet
Primal hunger
longing remains
Insatiable appetite
physical pain
Burning embers
remnants of fire
Sexual napalm
object of desire
Forbidden love
forever apart
A distant memory
affair of the heart

The Quest

Follow the light
into the storm
Where love awaits
and passion is born
The quest ignites
a blazing fire
Satiated only
by your desire
A song, a dance
romance sparked
Combustible heat
a flaming heart
Forever lover
from the start
Entwined as one
never to part

When Cupid Strikes

Love is a challenge
a roll of the dice
Frequently fragile
akin to thin ice
Love can be measured
a day at a time
For some a life sentence
a passionate crime
Love is a fire
a red-hot flame
Once an inferno
you won't be the same
Love is consuming
an arrow to the heart
A prisoner of cupid
you'll know from the start

Love Bandit

Hijacked heart
carnal delight
A desperado
thief in the night
Butterfly kisses
a tender embrace
He's a scoundrel
beware the chase
Utterly smitten
lured by charm
Into his lair
oblivious of harm
Flames of passion
emotional storm
Target of affection
beyond reform
Fully seduced
prisoner for life
The bandit of love
made me his wife

Against the Odds

From the beginning
you were the one
My partner in crime
the smoking gun
An imperfect couple
with a messy past
We forged ahead
determined to last
Ups & downs
mountains to climb
Weathered each storm
the test of time
Better together
love from the start
United we stand
til death do us part

Dedicated to my wonderful husband Adam Sherban

My Forever

You entered the room
handsome and strong
With pride & confidence
aware you belonged
A valiant knight
I knew from the start
You were the one
who stole my heart
Eye to eye
unable to speak
Our silence broken
a kiss on my cheek
Forever began
as you lead me away
Trajectory altered
forever that day

DATE NIGHT

Love & romance
that's all fine
Date night rocks
a bottle of wine
Shared with hubby
my one true love
A little bit chubby
he fits like a glove
BFFs, lovers, & friends
Partners forever
us til the end

THE CODE

Sacred union
pledge made
Equal partners
love brigade
Wedded bliss
utopian throes
Intimate dance
domestic tango
Marital code
love & lust
Encrypted passion
romance a must
United hearts
imperfect pair
Co-conspirators
family affair
Mr. & Mrs.
nucleus plus
Conjugal bond
forever us

Drowning

Lost in your gaze
dark as the sea
Deep like the Ocean
hauntingly free
Pulled by the tide
wind sets sail
Into your arms
a wanton jail
Drenched in longing
breakers divide
Emotions conflict
waves collide
Drowning in misery
grasping for air
Silently praying
soul in despair
Final Hail Mary
our hearts released
Into eternity
forever in peace

Mr. Wrong

Forever love
yours to pursue
Is he borrowed
or someone new
Perhaps a liar
adored by all
Stud or stallion
make the call
Gifts with jewels
affection withheld
Trips abroad
name misspelled
Spends the day
absent nights
Smooth operator
fight or flight
Rivulet of tears
salty cheeks
Pleasure sparse
sadness speaks
Smoke & mirrors
bittersweet
Mr. Wrong
man's a cheat

Toxic Love

Eyes wide open
feet on the floor
Lightning strikes
rocks your core
Real Slim shady
fake Don Juan
Toxic love story
fate gone wrong
Tunnel vision
cracks appear
Sirens blaring
danger nears
Common sense
out the door
Second chance
final encore
Conflicted heart
imperilled soul
Resolve wavers
swallowed whole
Radioactive
love gone bad
Run, don't walk
man's a cad

The Love Story

We embark on life
innocence in tow
Hopes & dreams
our seeds to sow
Rose-coloured lenses
what could go wrong
Our heart bestowed
to whom it belongs
Our pathways merge
two becomes one
My Ying, your Yang
our story's begun
Love is forever
or so we're told
Til death do us part
our plan to grow old
Life takes a twist
a fork in the road
One becomes two
we begin to erode
Our universe shatters
like broken glass
Our cosmic love story
wasn't meant to last

Emotional Warfare

Beyond the grave
aria's ring
Restless spirits
lost souls sing
Tragic love stories
forlorn wails
Hidden passions
untold tales
Scores to settle
secrets revealed
Private matters
affairs concealed
Dearly departed
legacies of love
Stones cast
signs from above
Behind the shroud
truth laid bare
Broken hearts
emotional warfare

Life according to "L"

Laugh daily, deep from the tummy
Lift up others, doesn't cost money
Lust nightly, with fire & passion
Light spiritually, it's still in fashion
Live in the moment, undeterred
Listen earnestly, absorb what is heard
Liberate from convention, personal growth
Learn for tomorrow, make it your oath
Let go of the past, it's set in stone
Leave no regrets, nothing to bemoan
Leap into the future, despite uncertainty
Love unconditionally, into eternity

Age of Innocence

Children smiling
toothy grins
Faces beaming
life begins
Tiny dancers
fountains & puddles
Laughter ringing
soggy cuddles
Trikes & bikes
skinned little knees
Boundless energy
climbing trees
Building sandcastles
babes at the beach
Fun with play dates
a delighted screech
Young & innocent
a mind to teach
Eyes wide open
the stars within reach

Mind Over Matter

Failure is subjective
a benchmark of dread
Negative images
clutter your head
Wasted energy
not well spent
A futile effort
cause to lament
Perception rules
loss turns to win
Silver linings
on every spin
Shifting perspective
from deep within
A positive attitude
good place to begin

Rite of Passage

Youth flies by
time disappears
Milestones pass
old age nears
Memory's sharp
futures unclear
Young at heart
must persevere
Beauty fades
body transforms
Wrinkles appear
hard to conform
Maturity level
a state of mind
Retirement plans
redefined
Path paved
lessons learned
Golden Years
passage earned

Life's Journey

A life lived
absent regrets
Special friends
i'll never forget
People I've met
along the way
Some move on
others may stay
Bonds forged
forever I pray
A gift received
not to betray
Love found
time measured
So profound
eternally treasured

The Exchange

Words wielded
thoughts relayed
Wisdom shared
emotion displayed
Ideas heard
sentiments spoken
Unique concepts
debate provoking
Angry outbursts
lethal darts
Regretful tears
forgiveness starts
Verbal exchanges
delivered with class
Visual contact
a bit of sass
Expression noted
message clear
Next topic
new frontier

No Regrets

Life goes quickly
no time to lose
Absent do-overs
can't pick or choose
Karma's a bitch
lightning fast
Right or wrong
deeds gone past
Pedal to the metal
full speed ahead
Play like the devil
knock em dead
Love til it hurts
explore each turn
Mourn what's lost
give in return
Depart in style
lest we forget
A life well lived
is not with regret

Personal Currency

A prosperous life
gifts bestowed
Not for purchase
beware the show
Designer clothes
trendy styles
Charitable causes
more worthwhile
Bells & whistles
fit for a King
Nature's canvas
more my thing
Love & tenderness
a warm embrace
Family & friends
can't replace
Inner peace
an open heart
Monetary value
off the chart
Intangible assets
all can afford
Lead with benevolence
reap the reward
A perfect life
not so fast
Blessings & benefits
unsurpassed

Giving Back

A simple gesture
extended hand
Community spirit
take a stand
Generous deeds
volunteer time
Underprivileged
not a crime
Fellow humans
broken souls
Restore dignity
collective goals
Offer shelter
medical care
Nutritious meals
clothes to wear
Basic necessities
mitigate strife
Second chance
gift of life
Exercise empathy
moral support
Human decency
not a spectator sport

It's a Wrap

Restless drifter
been around
Turbulent life
upside down
Twists & turns
one-way streets
Lessons learned
faced defeat
Loved hard
heart broken
Town crier
outspoken
Cocktail hour
hold the tea
Smokin ciggies
not for me
Party favours
pass the hat
Family drama
over that
Lady boss
cut the crap
Travel bug
peg the map
Just like that
in a snap
Piper paid
life's a wrap

OutKast

Social missteps
internet fails
Road to perdition
network jails
Verdict rendered
tried & convicted
Public justice
unrestricted
Personal defects
future foiled
Deep-sixed
image soiled
Crash-landing
overblown
Frenemy territory
hostile zone
Solo journey
fall from grace
Cancel culture
life erased

ONE OF A KIND

Life is a roadmap
master plan
A greater power
immortal man
Conception to birth
Almighty decides
Genetic composition
totally classified
Personal circumstance
not your choice
Situational events
use your voice
Moral fiber
persona forms
Intestinal fortitude
weather the storm
Fiery spirit
shining star
Prized heirloom
raise the bar
One of a kind
prodigal son
God's creation
the chosen one

Perfect World

Equal rights
beyond grassroots
Men & women
don't dispute
Pride over prejudice
a freedom call
Sexual identity
acceptance for all
Eradicate racism
focus the lens
A rainbow of hues
bigotry ends
Society's vulnerable
kindness prevails
Lead with empathy
blaze the trails
Spread compassion
move with stealth
Personal currency
emotional wealth
Love with impunity
open the door
In a perfect world
peace over war

The Blast

Magnificent life
checkered past
Chilling events
destiny cast
Fresh start
secrets hidden
Pages turned
entry forbidden
Polished façade
tarnished soul
Master chameleon
pigeon-holed
Delicate issues
collision course
Scores settled
no remorse
Intricate web
factual mess
Blasts from the past
laid to rest

PERSONAL VALUE

The price of life
value measured
Deemed important
what is treasured
The almighty dollar
demon disguised
A necessary evil
word to the wise
Gems & Jewels
designer Flare
Don't be fooled
principles beware
Flashy cars
bikes & boats
Material goods
not much to gloat
Family & Friends
forever true
Absent judgement
only love you

Cheers

A lush's nectar
fruit of the vine
Ripened grapes
an ode to wine
Shiraz works best
calms my nerves
Empty that bottle
fetch the reserve
Keep it flowing
bring me the best
Let's share a toast
be my guest
Cheers to you
and here's to us
Nature's gift
a definite plus

The Lesson

A day in the life
of anyone but you
Provides a narrative
a window to peer thru
A pair of shoes
belonging to another
To walk a mile
for a sister or brother
Someone's hardship
becoming your own
Your lesson learned
about casting a stone

POINT OF ORIGIN

Big city girl
little to boast
Small town roots
valued most
A global citizen
blessed indeed
Country to country
a desire to feed
Bucket list items
hidden gems
Historical treasures
many new friends
Poems inspired
notes to compare
Memories created
stories to share
A fortuitous life
different from many
Wanderlust heart
adventures are plenty
Regardless the path
wherever I roam
Point of origin
is always home

C-Town Central

Good ol' days
C-town vibe
Party central
705
Blazing fires
name the pit
Blunts burning
take a hit
Ditch drinking
tokers' bridge
Box of 2-4
raid the fridge
Silver Queen
Nellie Lake
Abitibi
congregate
Fishing, camping
squad patrol
Weekend benders
no control
Thibs, Chamandys
rock the house
London Tavern
word of mouth

After hours
stagger home
Walk of shame
never alone

Dedicated to every single "Cochranite" who was fortunate enough to live this wonderful truth!

Rise Up

Lead by example
dare to be bold
Societal norms
break the mold
Shatter glass houses
pulverize stones
Defy hypocrites
flex your backbone
Eliminate barriers
blast open doors
Self-investment
own the floor
Remain humble
rise above
Transcend limits
show the love
Shine your light
pave the trail
Steer your ship
set the sail
Ignore the noise
beware the crowd
Lead with integrity
forever be proud

The "Millennial"

High on a pedestal
just out of reach
Teetering, tottering
figure of speech
Raised bar
trajectory set
No debate
blood & sweat
Intrusive spotlight
frosted lens
Sink or swim
must contend
Double digits
breaking bank
Strategic planning
maximum rank
Success driven
fever pitch
Master class
generation rich

Dedicated to my brilliant son Justin Moorehead

Team Green

Broken planet
global game
Mutual burden
share the blame
Damaged ozone
plague inflicted
Air polluted
folks conflicted
Carbon emissions
foot off the gas
Renewable energy
produce en masse
Collective effort
deep divide
Achilles' heel
magnified
Sustainable living
go Team Green
Next generation
lifestyle clean

Printed in Canada